Today's Superst★rs
Entertainment

Alicia Keys

by Geoffrey M. Horn

GARETHSTEVENS
GS
PUBLISHING
A Member of the WRC Media Family of Companies

Please visit our web site at: www.garethstevens.com
For a free color catalog describing our list of high-quality books and
multimedia programs, call 1-800-542-2595 (USA) or 1-800-387-3178 (Canada).

Library of Congress Cataloging-in-Publication Data

Horn, Geoffrey M.
    Alicia Keys / by Geoffrey M. Horn.
        p. cm. — (Today's superstars. Entertainment)
    Includes bibliographical references and index.
    ISBN-13: 978-0-8368-4233-3 (lib. bdg.)
    ISBN-10: 0-8368-4233-2 (lib. bdg.)
    1. Keys, Alicia—Juvenile literature.   2. Singers—United States—
Biography—Juvenile literature.   I. Title.
ML3930.K39H37   2005
782.42164'092—dc22
[B]   2005046496

This edition first published in 2006 by
Gareth Stevens Publishing
A Weekly Reader® Company
1 Reader's Digest Road
Pleasantville, NY 10570-7000 USA

This edition copyright © 2006 by Gareth Stevens, Inc.

Editor: Jim Mezzanotte
Art direction and design: Tammy West
Picture research: Diane Laska-Swanke

Photo credits: Cover, p. 12 © Kevin Mazur/WireImage.com; pp. 5, 17, 18
Photofest; pp. 7, 22, 27 © Frank Micelotta/Getty Images; p. 8 © Gregg
DeGuire/WireImage.com; p. 11 © Johnny Nunez/WireImage.com; p. 15
© Kevin Winter/Getty Images; p. 20 © Stephen Shugerman/Getty Images;
p. 25 © Vince Bucci/Getty Images; p. 28 © Matthew Simmons/Getty Images

Printed in the United States of America

2 3 4 5 6 7 8 9 11 10 09 08 07

Contents

Chapter 1

Hotter Than July

In the music world, the summer of 2001 was the Summer of Alicia. At the time, Alicia Keys was only twenty years old. Wearing her hair in cornrows, she looked more like a college girl than a pop superstar. But when she played the piano and sang her songs, she wowed everyone who heard her.

By that summer, Alicia had been trying to make it big in the music business for almost four years. J Records put out *Songs in A Minor* in June 2001. It was Alicia's first album. Suddenly, Alicia Keys was unstoppable.

She charmed Oprah Winfrey. She impressed Jay Leno. By early July, *Songs in A Minor* was the best-selling album in the United States. A month later, "Fallin',"

Charting the Hits

Want to know who's hot and who's not? A good way to find out is to read *Billboard* magazine. For more than sixty years, *Billboard* has been charting the top U.S. hits. Today, *Billboard* puts together many different music and video charts. The magazine tracks sales of pop, R&B, rap, Latin, jazz, and many other kinds of music.

Alicia may be young, but she already has the skills and smarts of a seasoned performer.

the album's first single, topped the pop charts. The R&B and hip-hop charts? Alicia was tops there, too.

Layers of Sound

Like all of Alicia's best songs, "Fallin'" has many layers of sound. First, there is the voice. Alicia's voice rises and falls, sobs and wails, stumbles and soars. She doesn't sound like a twenty-year-old kid. She sounds like a soul singer from the 1960s or 1970s — like Aretha Franklin or Stevie Wonder, one of her heroes.

Next, there is the piano playing. It's not just a simple chord or two. Alicia knows and loves the keys. She's had years of training at the keyboard. She really knows how to play.

You can also hear other voices behind Alicia's lead vocal. These backing vocals tell us what the singer is going through and what she's thinking. At one point in the song, Alicia's voice and the backing vocals

Fact File

Alicia says one of her favorite Stevie Wonder songs is "They Won't Go When I Go." It was recorded in 1974 and opens with a beautiful piano solo.

weave together on the word "fallin'."
The voices fall like a heavy chain, as
the pain of love pulls Alicia down.

Bass and drums add muscle to the mix.
It all sounds old school, but with a taste
of hip-hop to keep it fresh. This recipe
took Alicia to the top of the charts in
2001. A similar recipe worked on *The
Diary of Alicia Keys*, which came out in
2003. *Diary* was Alicia's second chart-
topping album.

Stevie Wonder
is one of Alicia's
musical heroes.
The two performed
together at the
2004 MTV Video
Music Awards.

Alicia earned many honors in 2001, including *Billboard* Music Awards as Female Artist of the Year and New Female Artist.

Thriving on Success

How far can Alicia go? Music insiders think she has the talent and drive to go as far as she wants. "Some young performers get paralyzed by fame," notes Robert Hilburn of the *Los Angeles Times*. But Alicia is different. Hilburn says she "thrives on success, constantly setting new goals." He calls her most recent shows "dazzling."

In Hell's Kitchen

Alicia was born January 25, 1981, in New York City. Her birth name was Alicia Augello Cook. She didn't become Alicia Keys until she signed her first record deal.

Alicia's father is Craig Cook, an African American. Her mother is Terri Augello, a white woman who is part Italian. Cook left Augello when Alicia was two years old. "I do know who my father is," she told a writer for *Rolling Stone* magazine. "He didn't live with me. He didn't raise me. I don't call him Dad."

Terri Augello wanted to be an actress. But she had to support Alicia. She took a job as a paralegal. "Growing up, we didn't have anybody but each other to survive in the city," says Alicia.

Alicia never felt she had to choose between black and white, like some children of mixed race. She says her mother's closest friends were African Americans and Latinos. Alicia grew up feeling she could be part of any group.

Tough Town

Terri and Alicia lived on the west side of Manhattan. Their block was in Hell's Kitchen, a rough area between Times Square and the Hudson River. Here, Alicia saw the seamy side of New York City. "Runaways, loonies … everyone who was an outcast was right there," Alicia recalls.

Alicia still has mixed feelings about her hometown. "It's hard and it's dark and it's rough. Any moment, any corner, something is just dying to lure you in and bring you down."

Fact File

Hell's Kitchen has been a rough place for a long time. *The New York Times* called it "probably the lowest and filthiest in the city." The paper made this statement in 1881 — one hundred years before Alicia was born.

Early Lessons

Alicia began piano lessons at an early age. Her teachers used the Suzuki (suh-ZOO-kee) method. Suzuki was a violin player and teacher who lived in Japan. He believed the best way for children to learn music is by starting young.

Children learn to speak by copying people around them. Most kids can understand and say hundreds of words before they can read a single one. Suzuki believed kids could learn to play music the same way. In the Suzuki method, they first play by ear. They watch and listen. Then, they copy what the teacher does. They don't begin to read music until much later.

Alicia's lessons weren't cheap. She knew her mom had a hard time paying for them. She offered to give up the lessons, but her mother said no. "Quit what you like," Terri told her daughter. "But you're not quitting piano."

Family ties are important to Alicia. Her mother (second from left), godfather (second from right), and grandmother joined with her in 2003 to celebrate the release of her second album.

Music in New York City

New York City has many musical traditions. Broadway musicals are performed in the theater district, near Hell's Kitchen. Tin Pan Alley is another New York tradition. Before rock and roll, many pop songs were written in this part of the city. Early R&B classics were written and recorded in the Brill Building, not far from where Alicia grew up. Latin music also has a home in New York City.

Alicia took voice lessons in Harlem. This part of New York holds an important place in the city's musical history. Harlem was at its peak in the 1930s. At that time, Cab Calloway and Billie Holiday were top performers. The Cotton Club was the city's hottest nightspot. Alicia included a tribute to Harlem's golden era in her 2005 tour.

Alicia starred on the MTV Video Music Awards show and was honored as Best New Artist of 2001.

But New York also has a positive side. For Alicia, the city is a source of energy and passion. "New York is my home," she says. "It's where I grew up. It's where I live. It's where I love. And it's where I learned my biggest lessons."

True Emotion

Music has been an important part of Alicia's life for as long as she can remember. "I've had a deep love for music since I was four," she told a *Rolling Stone* reporter. "Music came before everything, everything, everything. It just meant more than anything ever meant. I would risk everything for it."

She listened to all kinds of music when she was growing up — classical, jazz, and rock, and artists such as Marvin Gaye, Jimi Hendrix, and Prince. She learned from it all. She says she responded to any music that had "that thing — that true emotion." That's what making music means to her. "For real. Not for fun. Not for money. For real."

Fact File

When Alicia was a teenager, Marvin Gaye was one of her favorite singers. His best-known album, *What's Going On*, came out in 1971.

Chapter 3

Finding Her Own Voice

Alicia started piano lessons at the age of seven. Later, she took singing lessons at a community center in Harlem.

When Alicia hit her teens, she began writing her own songs. She calls "I'm All Alone" the first good song she ever wrote. She was fourteen when she wrote it. Her grandfather had just died. "I was so upset," she recalled, "because they had to call 911 over and over before the ambulance ever came. He was dyin', and no one was there to help him."

As a teenager, she attended Professional Performing Arts High School. The school is

Fact File

Professional Performing Arts High School was started in 1990. Alicia is one of its most famous graduates. Britney Spears also took courses there. So did actress Clare Danes and dancer Clyde Archer.

Asleep at the Keys

In 2005, a writer asked Alicia if she had ever been so tired
she fell asleep at the keyboard. "Oh, man, this is funny," she
answered. "When I was younger, studying classical music,
I really had to put in the time. Three hours a day is not even
nice — you have to put in six. I had to do all these dreaded
scales. And out of the blue, I'd become exhausted. So there
were plenty of times I woke up at the piano." The same thing
sometimes happened when she dreamed about a song. She
would get out of bed and go to her keyboard. She'd play for
a while, until she reached a stopping point. "I'd lay my head
down to think," she said, "and boom, it was morning."

Alicia has boosted her career
with performances on programs
such as *The Tonight Show* with
Jay Leno.

located in the same Hell's Kitchen area where she grew up. At Performing Arts, students performed all kinds of music, including classical, opera, and R&B. "We did a little bit of everything," Alicia says.

False Starts

Alicia finished high school at the age of sixteen. She applied to Columbia University, in New York City. The college offered her a scholarship, and she accepted. In the fall of 1997, Alicia entered Columbia as a college freshman. She didn't stay very long.

College work wasn't the problem. Alicia's talent was. Word about this hot young singer was getting around. In the 1990s, record companies were paying big bucks for young talent — the younger the better. Alicia didn't want to miss her chance to be a superstar.

Fact File

Alicia loves the music of Nina Simone. Simone died in 2003. People called her the "High Priestess of Soul." Like Alicia, she played piano while she sang.

Before She Was Famous

Songs in A Minor was Alicia's first full album. But it wasn't her first recorded music. Alicia sang "The Little Drummer Girl" on a So So Defs Christmas album in 1996. Her "Dah Dee Dah (Sexy Thing)" appeared on the *Men in Black* soundtrack album in 1997. Three years later, she sang "Rock Wit U" on the *Shaft* soundtrack.

For Alicia, another step to stardom was an appearance at the 2001 What's Next in New Talent Party. *Teen People* magazine sponsored the event.

She dropped out of college and signed with Columbia Records.

The money was great. Alicia got a very good piano. At the age of seventeen, she moved into her own apartment in Harlem. But as an artist, she wasn't happy.

The record company sent her to work with people who didn't respect her views. They wanted to impose their ideas on her music. They figured Alicia was just a kid they could shape any way they wanted. Alicia knew better.

The music and cover photo for Alicia's first album show a strong, personal sense of style.

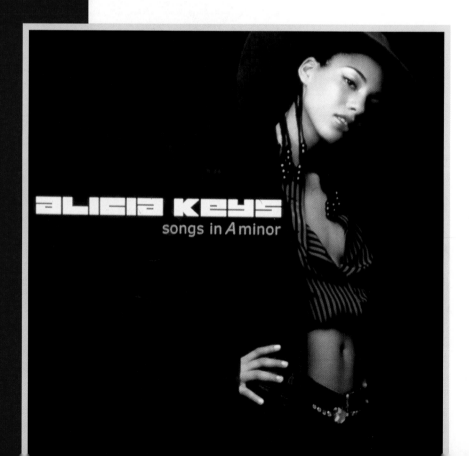

ALICIA KEYS
songs in *A* minor

Reasons to Believe

What does it take to make it big in the music business? Talent? Can't hurt. Faith in yourself? No doubt about it.

You need talent and self-confidence to make great music. To sell millions of records, however, you need something more. You need people who believe you can make it.

Throughout her life, Alicia has always had people who believed in her. The first person was her mother. "My mother is definitely my rock," Alicia says.

Another person was Jeff Robinson. Jeff is Alicia's manager. His brother, Conrad, was Alicia's coach when she first took voice lessons, in Harlem. Jeff met Alicia when she was fifteen.

Fact File

Songs in A Minor has sold more than ten million copies around the world.

19

Through Thick and Thin

Alicia's manager, Jeff Robinson, has stuck with her through good times and bad. "It's always been Jeff," she says. "It was Jeff when I was puttin' together my demos. It was Jeff when I didn't know how to produce nothin' and I was just tryin' to figure it out. I'd be in the bed, under the covers, tryin' to hide because I was depressed .... It was always Jeff. It wasn't nobody else."

For Jeff, the feeling was mutual. He says he likes working with up-and-coming artists. "The older artists are set in their ways," he complained to *Ebony*. "I want to work with those who are young and want to grow and develop. I don't believe in putting out an artist before their time."

Clive Davis and his newest superstar arrive at one of his famous pre-Grammy parties.

"My brother had asked me to come by and hear this young girl," Jeff told *Ebony* magazine. "He said she was pretty but very talented. I stopped by the studio one day and heard her sing and play the piano. … I was totally blown away."

"Jeff has believed in me from day one," Alicia says. "Through every up and down he's always been there for me."

An Ear for Talent

Alicia made a believer out of someone else, too. This person is a legend in the record business. His name is Clive Davis.

Long before Alicia was born, Davis was turning other people's talent into gold. He found Janis Joplin. He signed Whitney Houston. He revived the career of Carlos Santana. For twenty-five years, Davis led Arista Records. During that time, the label had two hundred number-one singles.

Alicia left Columbia Records for Davis's new record label, J Records. He was sure

Fact File

Clive Davis started J Records after he was forced out of Arista in 2000. By then, Davis was in his mid-sixties. His bosses at Arista thought he was too old!

Right, for a Change

Grammy voters picked right when they chose Alicia Keys as Best New Artist. But other deserving artists haven't been so lucky. Many famous music makers never won Best New Artist. Grammy voters somehow overlooked Bob Dylan, the Rolling Stones, and Stevie Wonder. How about Bruce Springsteen, Michael Jackson, or Madonna? Not a chance. Queen Latifah or Eminem? Forget it. All of them won later Grammy Awards, but not Best New Artist. The vote for Best New Artist of 1989 was one of the worst mistakes in Grammy history. The winner for that year was Milli Vanilli. A short time later, people learned that Milli Vanilli never performed a single note on their hit album, *Girl You Know It's True*. Their Grammy was taken away.

Clive Davis revived the career of Carlos Santana. Here the great guitarist performs with Alicia at a pre-Grammy party in 2005.

Alicia would be his next superstar. Davis has a great gift for building "buzz." Soon, the buzz machine was working overtime.

Each February, the music industry gives out its top prizes — the Grammy Awards. Grammy time is also a time for big parties. No party is bigger or more important than the one Davis gives each year. In 2001, he used his party to showcase his newest find. Alicia gave an incredible performance.

A year later, Alicia was back at the Grammy Awards ceremony. This time, however, she was one of the main prize winners. *Songs in A Minor* was voted Best R&B Album. "Fallin'" was Song of the Year and Best R&B Song. Alicia's singing on "Fallin'" won for Best Female R&B Vocal Performance. She also won for Best New Artist. Alicia received five Grammy Awards in one night, tying the record for a female artist.

Fact File

Two other women have won five Grammy Awards in one night. Lauryn Hill won five for her 1998 album *The Miseducation of Lauryn Hill*. So did Norah Jones, for her 2002 album *Come Away with Me*.

Chapter 5

Staying Power

The awards kept rolling in for Alicia in 2002. Black Entertainment Television (BET) named her Best New Artist, and she won two Teen Choice Awards. *People* magazine put her on its "50 Most Beautiful People" list. She also received a *Soul Train* Lady of Soul Award.

With *Songs in A Minor* riding high on the charts, Alicia hit the road with her band. Between concerts, she wrote songs. Her tour bus had a private space with a keyboard, so she could work while she traveled. When she stayed at a hotel, she had a keyboard in her room.

Fact File

Alicia says she wrote the song "Dragon Days" on the tour bus. She was missing her "special someone," and the days were "draggin'."

Got the Message?

Alicia's second album is called *The Diary of Alicia Keys.* Her full-length video is called *The Diary of Alicia Keys.* When she hit the road in 2005, her shows were called "The Diary Tour." When people went to her Web site, they saw the turning pages of a diary. It's all part of the way people in the music business sell an artist. If you hear the name Alicia Keys and instantly think "diary," her people have done their job well.

Alicia is a Grammy favorite. She won five Grammy Awards in 2002 and four more in 2005.

Much of her second album, *The Diary of Alicia Keys*, was written on tour.

Building on Success

Making a first album is tough. Making a second album is even tougher. A first album shows you can make a splash. A second album shows whether you have staying power.

With *Diary*, Alicia proved she was no one-hit wonder. Many songs on the album are as fine as anything on *Songs in A Minor*. On the hit single "You Don't Know My Name," she worked with Kanye West. On "If I Was Your Woman," she reworked an old R&B tune that was a hit for Gladys Knight. Other standout cuts are "Karma" and "If I Ain't Got You."

Diary didn't sell as many copies as *Songs in A Minor*. But among solo R&B artists, only Usher sold more records in 2004. The two sang together on one of the year's top singles, "My Boo."

Fact File

"My Boo" topped the very first *Billboard* chart of cell phone ring tones in November 2004.

New Soul

Alicia Keys, Jill Scott, Macy Gray, and some other artists
are often called "new soul" singers. They borrow some of
hip-hop's beats and rhymes. But they can work a tune like
the soul singers of the 1960s and 1970s. They sing about
today's problems, but they avoid the crude boasting and raw
language that many rappers use. "New soul" is sometimes
called "neo-soul" or "nu-soul."

**Alicia and Usher sang their smash
hit "My Boo" at the 2004 MTV
Europe Music Awards.**

Late in 2004, Alicia came out with *Tears for Water*, a book of song lyrics and poems.

Alicia took home four more Grammy Awards in February 2005. Grammy voters chose *Diary* as Best R&B Album. In 2004, she made about ten million dollars from concert tickets, CDs, and books. *Rolling Stone* placed her fiftieth on a list of top money makers.

Success is great. But for Alicia, music still comes first. "I definitely see myself growing in a lot of ways musically," she says. "This music thing, me and you, we're gonna do this for a long time."

Alicia strikes a studious pose at a book signing in West Hollywood, California.

Time Line

1981	Alicia Augello Cook is born in New York City on January 25.
1996	Sings "The Little Drummer Girl" on So So Defs Christmas album.
2000	Signs with Clive Davis's new label, J Records.
2001	*Songs in A Minor* tops the album charts and the song "Fallin'" is a number-one single.
2002	Wins five Grammy Awards, including Best New Artist.
2003	*The Diary of Alicia Keys* is Alicia's second number-one pop album.
2004	Usher and Alicia top the charts with "My Boo."
2005	Wins four more Grammy awards.
2007	Alicia appears in the Hollywood movies *Smokin' Aces* and the *The Nanny Diaries*.

Glossary

backing vocals — the extra voices that back up the lead singer.

charts — in the music business, lists of the most popular, best-selling artists.

chord — in music, a group of notes that are played at the same time.

demos — rough recordings made to show what a singer or songwriter can do.

Grammy — an award given out by the Recording Academy, a group of people who work in the music business. They vote on who should win.

lyrics — the words to a song.

paralegal — someone who isn't a lawyer but is trained to do some kinds of legal work.

R&B — short for rhythm and blues. At first, R&B was a mix of blues and dance rhythms. Today, it includes many kinds of African American pop music.

scholarship — money offered to help a student pay for college.

solo — in a piece of music, a part performed by a single voice or instrument.

soul — in music, a mix of R&B and gospel, a form of Christian religious music. Soul first became popular in the 1950s.

To Find Out More

Books

Alicia Keys. Blue Banner Biographies (series).
  John Bankston (Mitchell Lane)

The History of Motown. African American Achievers
  (series). Virginia Aronson (Chelsea House)

Working in Music and Dance. My Future Career
  (series). Margaret McAlpine (Gareth Stevens)

Videos

The Diary of Alicia Keys (Red Distribution) NR

Web Sites

Alicia Keys
www.aliciakeys.net
Photos, audio and video clips, and song lyrics

Billboard.com
www.billboard.com/bb/index.jsp
Music news and charts

In the Studio with Alicia Keys
www.aliciakeys.com/inthestudio/
Photos and video clips

Index

About the Author

Geoffrey M. Horn has been a fan of music, movies, and sports for as long as he can remember. He has written more than a dozen books for young people and adults, along with hundreds of articles on many different subjects. He lives in southwestern Virginia, in the foothills of the Blue Ridge Mountains, with his wife, their collie, and four cats. He dedicates this book to Harry Alan Davidson and Emily Louise Neuwirth.